Ghetto Love
Part 2
My version
Of
Sex, Pain, Love
&
The Lord

I0200986

Sedelia Gardner

Avid Readers Publishing Group

Lakewood, California

Ghetto Love Part 2 My version Of

Sex, Pain, Love & The Lord

Avid Readers Publishing Group

http://www.avidreaderspg.com

ISBN-13: 978-1-61286-118-0

Printed in the United States

Ghetto - *A ghetto is literally a poor or dangerous neighborhood. Or used to refer to the poor African American neighborhoods of the city. The slums of the city or the dirtiest place to live.*

Love -*to feel tender affection for somebody .Or to feel a romantic and sexual desire and longing for somebody.*

Ghetto love *– The secret dangerous dirty African American attraction that happens between two people.*

Part one

Sex

Once of the most creative things on earth were you can express your feeling for someone without using words.

Does it feel good to you?

Slide in slowly

And tell me what you feel

Is it soft?

Is it wet?

Is it warm inside?

Does it feel good to you?

Move in slow motion

And tell me what you feel

Is that the spot?

Is that the way

Is that the best?

Does it feel good to you?

Whisper to me

And tell me what you feel

Is it good?

Is it yours?

Is it tight?

I feel your grip

Now tell me what you feel

Are you there?

Are you almost

Are you about to

Does it feel good to you?

Sedelia Gardner

2

Cream & sugar

I hear the drips as the coffee begins to brew

It's early but not too early to have a sip or two

I'm just wondering will you be having

Cream & sugar

The strong aroma begins to fill the air as the coffee continues to brew

I can see the steam rise up from my cup

Will you be having cream & sugar?

You take your finger and place it in my cup

And twirl it around making the aroma stronger

Almost more than I can bare

But I am still wondering

Will you be having cream & sugar?

I watch your undecided look as you choose what to do

Sugar is sweet but sometimes cream is sweeter

So you stir in your sugar and blend in your cream

Lick your fingers

As I lay back for you to enjoy

Your morning cup of coffee

Sedelia Gardner

Uncharted Waters

*Uncharted waters come on and take ride in them you
don't need a crew there is*

*Only room for one don't worry about a map just let my
moans be your guide*

*Uncharted waters are sometimes rough to ride so you
can take your time and calm*

*The waters and let me relax so you can enjoy the
incoming tide*

*Uncharted waters come and lay back and drift into my
sweet abyss the journey may be*

*Long or it could be short it depends on the path you
take for this ride*

*Uncharted waters are nice and warm right now so
come dive deep and find that oyster*

With the hidden precious pink pearl trapped inside

*Uncharted waters there is no need to worry about
getting lost just relax and let my*

Moans be your guide

Sedelia Gardner

Liquid Asset

I have something precious

And it doesn't have a price tag on it

Many want it

And some even tired to buy it

And a few have even discovered it

And some have even tasted it

And a couple have even seen it

I have something precious

And some have a copy of it

And a few are as good as it

But none can compare to it

Even thou some many even look like it

It doesn't feel the same as it

It has my liquid asset in it

Come and play with it

I have something precious

Sedelia Gardner

Cool Breeze

This is tantalizing to my soul

This feeling I feel as the cool breeze rushes through my hair

I pull my skirt up just a bit

And adjust my thighs to feel the cool breeze pass through my hair

Low moans slip from between my lips

As the cool breeze blow through my hair

Sweat beads form across your brow

As the cool breeze flow through my hair

I lay back to enjoy

As you expel the cool breeze through my hair

Sedelia Gardner

African Fire

*What is that strange thing that waltz through the jungle
and dance to a*

*Beat of an unseen drummer creating unfamiliar
movement to virgins eyes that stir up the*

African fire

*Nectar it holds glistens like golden honey and is
sweeter than any red ripe pomegranate*

*King Solomon, Caesar and Mark Anthony are just a
few who were engulfed by the flames*

Of this African fire

*It graciously cascades its way through the cotton fields
fully clothed but unknowingly*

*Arouse the curiosity of her master thus creating
Mulottos just another breed that holds the*

Secrets of African fire

*A flame that began with the creation of Eve and have
been burning ever since its secrets*

*Have been past down from one brown skin mother to
her daughter on how to dance and*

Memorize the mind of many with her African Fire

Sedelia Gardner

Sweet Wine

I like mine a little dark and some like them white
But I prefer mines slightly chilled and while some
many prefer theirs at room temperature but the
young ones don't catch my attention at all
because I like mine a little aged ones that
will satisfy me just right let me get my
glass and began to pour I have been
waiting on this all day as I savor
the sweet drops upon my lips
nothing to add and no
complaints from me
and I sit back
and enjoy
my dark

S
W
E
E
T
WINE

Sedelia Gardner

You Watch

My hair dances in the wind freely like black silky
horses mane

And you watch

My body moves in ways you never seen feels like ocean
waves crashing up on the shores

And you watch

My breast dance for you to the beat of your drum
jumping like roasting popcorn seeds

And you watch

My sweat begins to run down my body covering me in
an Amazon waterfall

And you watch

My grip begins to get tighter on you it feels like a
python squeezing her prey

And you watch

My eyes close gently and I am set free floating in gentle
winds like a leaf

And you watch

My head goes back and we both let out a familiar
moan that echoes through the room

And you watch

And I watch

You

Sedelia Gardner

9

No Panties on

*I feel your eyes all over me it's like you're making
love to me as I make my way across the crowded room
curiosity has taken hold of you I can tell by the smile
on your face that you're wondering*

If I have no panties on

*As my hips swing your way and I can tell your eyes are
following my every move so I stop and move a slower
and the view of my ass is teasing your curiosity as you
being to wonder*

If I have no panties on

*I adjust myself in my chair and I move my legs a little
so you can see her I know you like it the way your
smiling back at me now your curiosity makes you want
to meet her maybe it can happen now that you know*

I have no panties on

Sedelia Gardner

Rose

I am wrapped up tight

Bind together like the unopened petals on a rose bud

I let your touch slowly unravel my petals

*The sweet aroma from the petals begin to enlighten
your senses*

And please your inner soul

The desire to embrace more is right there

At the very tip

And I am barely open

Sedelia Gardner

Voice

Whisper in my ear and let the words flow

Let the vibrations travel to excite my soul

My eyes began to close because you are not here

But my body is longing for a voice over the phone

Talk softly to me and the let the words flow

So they can ripple over my body

To make it seem like you are touching me

It won't last long

Because you are just a voice over the phone

Speak my name and let it flow

So I can think that you want me and believe that you need me

I hold to my pillow

I think I will call it Joe

As I explode for a voice over the phone

Sedelia Gardner

Part 2

Pain

Pain causes scars no matter how little pain is felt sometimes the scar is even bigger and deeper than a person know.

Tears dry on their own

Let the raging river flow on its course

Crashing up against the rocks in its way

Destroying anything that stands in it way

Over flow my banks and flood my valley

Let the tears roll down my cheeks

Because tears dry on their own

No need for sand bags

No need to build a dam to hold the water back

This is not the first time and won't be the last

But is will be the last time you see this river flow

I won't hold back let them fall

Because tears dry on their own

The river is almost done flowing

And the water reseeds from my banks

A little white path left on my face to let me know the path it took

The storm is over now and it's time to rebuild

Because tears dry on their own

Sedelia Gardner

Bedtime

It's bedtime and the sun is setting

And I stare out the window to watch it set

The moon is peering out between the dark clouds

It looks like a full one tonight

I turn back the bed sheets

So I can run my hands over your side of the bed

I can smell your cologne in the sheets

Even when you're not there

It's getting late and time is passing bye

I slip into your old tee-shirt

Just to pretend you're here holding me tight

The sun is about to rise

And the darkness of night fades away

And the only thing on your side of the bed is the scent of your cologne

I guess you forgot about your

Bedtime

Sedelia Gardner

Laugh at my pain

Here we go again

Same scenario just like it was before

No need to get mad anymore

All I can do now is laugh at my pain

The signs were there

Just like they were before

I chose to be blind and leave the open door

Now all I can do is laugh at my pain

No need to cry

I felt this all before

My soul still carries that open sore

All I can do now is laugh at my pain

Sedelia Gardner

You're not worth a tear

You're not worth a tear

But still I cry

Let the clouds move on and make my mind clear

Your love is a lie

But your touch feels good to me

Le the sunrays rain down on me and brighten my dark sky

I close my eyes the pain I don't want to see

You're not worth a tear

But still I cry

Let the rain drops pour down on me and wash away this smear

Your love to me you deny

But your kisses make it hard for me to hear

Let the winds blow my watery eyes dry

You're not worth a tear

But still I cry

Sedelia Gardner

How can you

How can you love me?

When I don't even love myself

The way you talk to me

I don't mind

I don't know the difference

Because I don't even love myself

You call me everything but

The name I was born with

I don't mind

Maybe it's a game

I don't even know the difference

Because I don't even love myself

One hit two hit three hits then more

It's okay baby because

I don't even feel the pain

How can you love me?

When I don't even love myself

Is this love that were making

I don't even know but that is what they call it

It's just something that last for a moment

So I could just have you close to me

How can you love me?

When I don't even love myself

Sedelia Gardner

Not Right

Dark chocolate, pecan, beige and once I even had
a touch of white all these different shades and I still
couldn't get it right

Strong arms ,weak arms, skinny and thick all wrapped
around me like tree roots it felt good for the moment
but it just didn't feel right

Dark brown , light brown, hazel, green and even a pair
of blue all these eyes trying to find my soul and I still
couldn't get it right

Waves, braids, dreads, afro, curly, grey and bald I ran
my fingers through them all in a bliss of happiness it
felt good but it just didn't feel right

Polo, brut, cool waters, drakkar, guess, joop, marc
Jacobs and even a drop of old spice just the smell
alone would set me on fire but I still couldn't get it
right

Short, tall, husky, stout, skinny, thug, hard worker,
playboy, comedian, rough rider each held my attention
for a brief moment it didn't last it just didn't feel right

So many different varieties so many combinations I
have tired they all felt good even if it was just for that
moment but I still couldn't get it right

Sedelia Gardner

Someone else's bed

From the very beginning

You told me this was a good thing

But you still fled to someone else's bed

You told me you could never find

Another to take my place

But you still fled to someone else's bed

Your words to me…

"I love you"

But you still fled to someone else's bed

In your arms I slept and cried

I supported you every way I could

But you still fled to someone else's bed

Someone came and found me

And placed me on their top shelf

While you still fled to someone else's bed

Spare me all your tears

I gave you everything but life itself

But you still fled to someone else's bed

Sedelia Gardner

I thank you

Other woman I thank you

*Being the other woman isn't easy to do when I'm at
home and he's with you so now I*

Become the other woman to

But I thank you

He is all yours

I thank you

His lies I no longer hear

I thank you

My eyes no longer cry

I thank you

I no longer have to argue and fight

I thank you

A weight has been lifted from me

And I thank you

Instead of feeling sad I feel relieved

I thank you

I can now sleep at night with a piece of mind

Other woman I thank you

Being the other woman isn't easy to do when you're at

home tonight and he's gone you now

Become the other woman to

Sedelia Gardner

360 degrees of separation

I hate you!

  Give me back my things!

Their mine!

  I brought them their mine!

Funny how things come apart when we start our 360
degrees of separation

What about this dog?

  Don't worry I will take him with me!

What about the kids?

  Don't worry I will see them when I can!

What about the rent, the bill, food?

  You better go get another job!

Funny how things don't mean nothing when we start
our 360 degrees of separation

Here take this ring!

  I'm going straight to the pawn shop!

I know I should have done your friend!

  Too bad because I did your girl!

Funny how things come out when we start our 360
degrees of separation

Sedelia Gardner

Over and Over

Another tear fall
From my eyes
And it rolls down my cheek
To follow the invisible trail
Left behind from the ones
That traveled there before
It reaches the bottom
Falls off the cliff
Floats in thin air with no wings
Splash

Here we go again
Another replay of yesterday
The same thing
Over and over

My heart beats
A little faster now
I can feel it lift up
Suspended in thin air
And press against my chest
The same pain
I felt yesterday
I feel it all over again
Then my heart falls
Splash

Here we go again
Another replay of yesterday
The same thing
Over and Over

Sedelia Gardner

Hollow Box

*And I sat under the weep willow tree holding my
hollow box*

*And I shed my tears until they over flowed my hollow
box*

*And they ran over and dropped into the soil below to
fill a hollow box*

*And my tears gave life to the seed below that was
packed in the hollow box*

*And that seed reminded me that there is life after pain
in my hollow box*

*And the leaves stretch up and embraced the light and
pulled it in my hollow box*

*And I sat under the weeping willow tree hold my new
life in my hollow box*

Sedelia Gardner

Nobody's Perfect

Nobody's perfect here

You sit you think you decide then you make a choice

Just like I do

And not all of them are right

You're not perfect that's why some of them are wrong

Nobody's perfect here

You sit you think you wonder then you cry

Just like I do

And not all of those tears are tears of joy

You're not perfect that's why sometimes you cry alone

Nobody's perfect here

You sit you think you breathe then you bleed

Just like I do

And not all of those scars heal

You're not perfect that's why some of your choices left a scar

Because nobody's perfect here

Sedelia Gardner

My Cup Runneth Over

And this empty cup sits in front of me

But something about the emptiness has a hold on me

My eyes begin to burn as the pain replay inside of me

The water forms in my eyes as my dreams slip away from me

And this empty cup still sits in front of me

The dam in my eyes began to break as the emptiness escapes me

The water slips from my eyes as the pain floats away from me

The empty cup begins to fill up with the river of pain that leaves me

This empty cup is now filled with pain and it no longer has a hold on me

And my cup runneth over

Sedelia Gardner

Shadows

I let the shadows chase me because I am headed to the light up ahead

I let the shadows dance a circle around me because there is light shining above my head

I let the shadows talk to me and in return I tell them about the light up ahead

I let the shadows crowd me in a dark room because the light is still bright in my head

So I let the shadows come because there is always light up ahead

Sedelia Gardner

Fortress

*I'm here in this fortress I was born with and there is
only one ruler here and that's me*

If I scream I scream alone

If I cry I cry alone

*But sometimes I drift off to a peaceful dream there are
moments like that when I don't feel alone*

*If you could look behind these castle walls that took
years for me to build*

*You will see the scars of many battles and many wars
that my fortress has stood against*

*I won some battles and lost some battles but my
fortress just kept on beating*

*Every boulder that fell from it I just replaced it with a
stronger one*

*Now it consist of a matrix of chaos and hell locked
deep inside a keyless chest*

Sedelia Gardner

I'm Rolling

I'm rolling off the back of loves sweet melodies

And the tears I cry reminds my soul that I won't survive

So I float across the sky replaying

Loves memories in my mind

The tears dry up so my soul can breathe

I'm rolling off the back of loves sweet melodies

They keep my heart beating so my soul will survive

So I hold on to the melodies so the tune can keep replaying

Forming love thoughts in my mind

The smiles reappear so my soul can breathe

I'm rolling off the back of loves sweet melodies

And this new tune that I hymn reminds me of the life I have left so I know I will survive

Giving me a new hope in my mind

And now that I know your gone memories of you are not worth replaying

The tears are all dried up and I can now breathe

I'm rolling off the back of loves sweet melodies

Sedelia Gardner

To whom it may Concern

Just because I miss you

Doesn't mean I want you back

Just because you cross my mind from time to time

Doesn't mean I need you back in my life

Just because I can admit I still care for you

Doesn't mean I love you

Just because I still have your picture in a frame

Doesn't mean I want you here

Just because my child may remind me of you

Doesn't mean I want to be with you

Just because I get lonely sometime

Doesn't mean I can't go on without you

To whom it may concern

I just hope you are doing just fine

I have learned to keep moving on without you

Sedelia Gardner

Phone

Sitting here waiting

For the phone to ring

In my mind I should know better

But my heart ignores the pain

As it tries to hold on to a memory of you and me

My heart keeps beating

To push away the pain

While I sit here waiting

For the phone to ring

Sedelia Gardner

Snow Bunny

*I see her eyes are as blue as the sea and her skin
is very fair are you attracted to her because of her
inability to think on her own makes you feel more like a
man as she dance around you like a snow bunny*

*Maybe I said to much or I did the job that you should
have done I know my skin will always be the perfect
brown it won't change with the season like your snow
bunny*

*I see her mouth it barely opens so you can have all the
control to say what you like does that make you feel
more like man as she dance around you like a snow
bunny*

*Maybe I was too hard I was able to take the good with
bad I even pulled out an umbrella to shelter you as
I stood in the winds and danced in the rain that part
of me won't ever change unlike the fur on your snow
bunny*

Sedelia Gardner

Part three

Love

Is it possible to have a love affair with someone that will last forever because they are blind to all your imperfection and only see your beauty the beauty you didn't even see or knew was there? And even thou you look in the mirror day after day you still can't see what they see. It's like they are wearing a blind fold everyday they are with you. So this section I dedicate to Dwight Gordon thank you for your wearing a blind fold.

Better Half

I floated among the white clouds in the sky looking for my better half

Wandered in the deep green forest walking around searching for you

I even walked across the endless hot dessert sands and searched under stones

And I dived deep into the blue sea and swam the endless ocean

Climbed the highest mountains and screamed out your name

Looking for my better half

I have come across many pretending they were you

Pretending to love me and acting like they cared for me

Blinding and torturing my soul making it hard for me to believe

My better half was still out there and he was looking for me

There you are my heart said as I looked into your eyes

The ache in my chest as my heart stopped for you

It was the greatest pain I have ever felt in all my life

The reason I breathe

The reason behind my Mona Lisa smile

Is all because of you

The reason I am filled with joy and

My eyes fill up with joyful tears every time I think about us

My love

My life

My purpose to live

Nothing is more enjoyable than the burning in my soul that I have

For you

My better half

Sedelia Gardner

Kisses

If I could take back all the times I made you sad

And replace it with a kiss I would have to kiss you a hundred times

If I could take out my needle & thread and sew up the little hole I put in your heart

And replace it with a kiss I would have to kiss you a thousand times

If I could wipe away the tears I helped form in your eyes

And replace it with a kiss I would have to kiss you a million times

If I could take away all the pain I caused you

And replace it with a kiss I would have to kiss you a billion times

If I could make up for all the time I forgot to tell you I loved you

And replace it with a kiss I would have to kiss you a trillion times

If I could play back all the times you made me happy and laugh with joy

And replace it with a kiss you would have to kiss me a zillion times

Sedelia Gardner

My Love

My love today I thought about how my life

Would be without you and the pain was to

Great and that was just a thought my love

My love for you is bittersweet the pain of

Losing you is great but the joy and happiness

I now have with you is greater my love

My love just the mere thought of not having

You in my life cause my heart to ache with

A pain I can't stand to bare my love

My love for you that I feel I know when

It all began but the end is like the depths

Of the deep oceans I see no end to my love

Sedelia Gardner

This love

This love has me high about the clouds in the sky

I am next to the stars

With the moon beneath my feet and the sun sits

In the palm of my hand

This love glides me across the open waters

There I float under the blue skies

Going into the distant horizon

Unsinkable like a leaf floating across the sea

This love beams down on me like the sun rays upon the desert sands

Melting the skin from my body

And burning my soul with a heat

Only you can understand

Sedelia Gardner

Waiting on you

You came along and just let me be just me

I can have long hair, short hair, afro or braids

It just don't matter to you

Because my love for you is still there

Deep in my brown eyes sitting there waiting on you

I can be bold, I can be quiet, or a diva or the sassy little thing you like

My attitude can change like the wind

But just look deep in my brown eyes

And you can see my love is

Sitting there

Just sitting there waiting on you

I can gain a pound or two and even get a few gray hairs

And maybe get a few wrinkles to

And it just don't matter to you at all

Because my love for you will always be there

When you look deep in my brown eyes

You can see all my love that I have for you

Sitting there

Just sitting there waiting on you

Sedelia Gardner

Forever

And he spoke and everything came into existence and at that moment I was formed for you I twinkled in the moon lit skies with the stars above sitting there waiting on my forever

He gave me the gift of life as he breathe his essence into my soul and when our eyes met I knew that I had finally found my forever

He made you for me and me for you at the very moment he spoke everything into existence to find each other and come together as one forever

And as my body begins to age and my skin begins to winkle and the very essence he breathed into my body leaves this shell you will always be my forever

And he spoke and with those words he returned my essences to the skies above and there I sit twinkling with the stars waiting there again to be with my forever

Sedelia Gardner

Why you

*I looked over my left shoulder and reviewed the profiles
of all my past love's*

And I had no one to compare you to

*Your eyes are brown but it's a shade that I have never
seen before*

*Your skin is a shade of brown but it's a shade that has
never been matched with mine*

And it's all new to me

And I have no one to compare you to

*Your hands touch me in place I have been touched
many times before*

*But every touch of your hands makes me feel a little
different inside*

*Even when your lips touch mine they warm me in a
different way*

All of this is different to me

And I have no one to compare you to

*And I looked over my right shoulder and there you
stood all alone*

I have no one to compare you to

That's why I choose you

Sedelia Gardner

In your arms

*Seconds turn into minutes and then they turn into hours
and when the hours build up they turn into days and
after while they form weeks and then they turn into
months and now it's been some years that I have been
laying in your arms*

In your arms is where I lay

And in your arms in where I will stay

*A quick stare starts a moment and that turns into a
memory and then those turn into thoughts and after a
while those thoughts of you turn into dreams and that
starts a longing for you and a need for me to again lay
in your arms*

In your arms is where I lay

And in your arms in where I will stay

Sedelia Gardner

Your Kiss

Our eyes rejoice in the birth of a new day and as our eyes meet with the rising sun they then set with an embrace

Soft like the skin on a new born baby and it warms me like the rays coming from the shining sun

Small lines match up with mine as they touch each moving in an opposite direction but they form the perfect rotation

Two tongues begin to play a game of childhood tag as the twirl around in the dark cavern our embrace formed

Your kiss

Your kiss

Your kiss is what I call it

Sedelia Gardner

Loving Me

I arise from a blissful night of you loving me

Relaxed and chill was the outcome

I feel so chilled that hot lava couldn't burn my skin

You loving me fill a void that I have deep with in

It mingles with my soul and grabs hold of my heart

Until the beating stops

There is nothing more expensive than your love

And these is nothing known to men that can replace your love

It's just the way you love me so

I relax and prepare for another blissful night of you loving me

Sedelia Gardner

Closer to yours

And there you are across the room

Silently calling my lips

To come closer to yours

My feet are slowly lifted off the ground

As I float in a lustful thought

Dreaming of a love scene with just me and you

And there you are

My eyes locked in on yours

As you silently call my lips to come closer to yours

My mind starts to put together the perfect love scene

And my eyes began to undress you

As I move near

And here we are face to face

Silently calling my lips

To come closer to yours

Sedelia Gardner

Perfect Paradise

Pull me closer to you and wrap me in your arms

So we can share a love

Between me and you

As I nestle in your arms

I know what it feels like to lay in perfect paradise

I can hear the storms outside

But your love protects me from the rain

As I lay in your arms listening to the drops fall

I am lost in my perfect paradise

Let your lips touch mine

And the outsider arrows fall to the ground

This love is between me and you

My perfect paradise

Sedelia Gardner

Part 4

The Lord!

I refuse to let the residue of others or my past,

restrict me from receiving my future results!

HOW I SEE GOD

I see your presence like misty rain

Soft barely seen

But the moisture you leave behind

Lets me know you are there

I hear your voice like birds chirping

Sweet medleys

But even thou I don't understand the song they sing

You place it in my heart to understand the meaning

I feel your touch it's like cotton

Soft barely felt

But the feeling it leaves behind

Let me know you are there

I look to you and I see a light

Shining bright

But even thou I am not worthy the light shine on me still

You placed it in my heart to understand the meaning

Sedelia Gardner

Grateful

You fill me with hope

When I had no hope left

You held my hand

Even when I let yours go

I'm so grateful to have a father like you

You filled me with love

When I had no love left

You stood by my side

Even when my faith slipped away

I'm so grateful to have a father like you

You wiped my tears from my eyes

The ones that only you could see

You heard my cries

And I didn't even have to scream

I'm so grateful to have a father like you

You sacrificed your son for me

So that I may live

And even thou I still sinned

You still continued to bless me

I'm so grateful to have a father like you

Sedelia Gardner

I was made not to break

The water drips from my eyes
And are quickly absorb into my skin
The tears moisten my skin but it doesn't soften
Because I was made not to break

I was made in your image so
I know I was made not break
So I look to you

The shell of my body receives many blows
From my enemies
But my soul still remains untouched
Because I was made not to break

I am showered with you blessing so
I know I was made not break
So I look to you

The words from my enemies get thrown at me
From all angles and shake me but
My mind is at ease
Because I was made not to break

I am protected by your mercy so
I know I was made not break
So I look to you

Sedelia Gardner

Fly

I finally made it out of my cocoon
And I am doing all that I can
To spread my wings so that I
Can fly

I stumble and I fall
And sometimes my wings aren't strong enough
To hold me up but I still reach for
The sky

I am to strong and I am not weak
I maybe stubborn
But I refuse to sit down and die
When there is a small chance I
Can fly

I spread open my wings
And I spread them open with all my strength
I let go of the bondage that held me down
And I let the sweet winds of mercy carry me to
The sky

Sedelia Gardner

I'll Pray

I can't cry anymore so instead I'll just sit here and pray

I sit all alone in this dark room no one around

But I can feel his presence all around me

I can't cry anymore so instead I'll just here sit and pray

I can't even gather the strength to fuss and fight anymore

My shoulders are weighed down and I'm tired but

I can't cry anymore so instead I'll just sit here and pray

I look all around trying to figure out how this trouble entered my life

My heart is heavy and the pain is taking hold of me but

I can't cry anymore so instead I'll just sit here and pray

The screams won't come out no matter how hard I try

I try to cry but the tears refuse to fall

I can't cry anymore so instead I'll just sit here and pray

Sedelia Gardner

Your Blood Still Works

Through the dark and cloudy storms I stood alone

With my hands stretching out to you

And with you in my heart and I prayed

Through your precious blood I am saved

Because your blood still works

For those that believe

Darker than night itself and deeper than the see I sat alone

And I reached out for you as I cried

And with you in my heart I prayed

Through your precious blood I am saved

Because your blood still works

For those that believe

I prayed to you and the sun came out after the storm

And the sea I was drowning in was now a puddle beneath my feet

And I rejoiced with you in my heart and I sang

Through your precious blood I am saved

Because your blood still works

For those that believe

Sedelia Gardner

Your Hand

I wish I could see your hand in mine

As we travel together down the road

With your hand wrapped in mine

I wish I could feel your hand in mine

As I slip but quickly I am lifted up

As we travel together down the road

With your hand wrapped in mine

I wanted to see your hand in mine

The one that gives me strength

As we travel together down the road

With your hand wrapped in mine

I wanted to feel your hand in mine

But your presence in the midst alone is good enough

As we travel together down the road

With your hand wrapped in mine

Sedelia Gardner

Kneel to You

I stood before my enemies
With a back bone that refuse to break
And knees that refused to buckle
Lash after Lash my enemies put upon me
But still I stood
How could I even stand against them
When I have no one standing with me
I stood alone
And I refuse to be broken
Lash after Lash my enemies put upon me
My heart gave in
And my soul cried out
And I went on bended knees
I had to kneel before you first
So I could stop standing alone
I stand now with a back bone
That cannot be broken by man
And knees that only bend for my Father
The whip wraps around my body
But lashes I no longer feel
I had to kneel before you first
Before I could even stand at all

Sedelia Gardner

Shelter Me

Can you come and shelter me

From the storm

If just for a little while

I know there were times when I didn't come to you

*And I know there were times when I didn't call out to
you*

But today my burdens are more than I can bare

Lord you said you will never leave me

So I know you are there

So I ask

Can you come and shelter me

From the storm

If just for a little while

The tears keep falling and I feel my soul getting weak

No one is left in my corner but you

So now we finally speak

Here I am Lord I give it all to you

I tried it on my own

But I can't take another step without you

So I humble myself and ask

Can you come and shelter me

From the storm

If just for a little while

Sedelia Gardner

The Bridge

As

I see the other side

How bright the sun shines

As it rays dance around the green pastures

Just a finger tip away

How will I get there I wondered

As

I sit on the other side

How dark are the clouds around me

As the rain pour down on me

As I look at the sun just a finger tip away

How will I get there I wondered

As

I walk towards the other side

How a bridge was forming beneath my feet with your

WORD

As the bridge kept forming the sun was closer than just

a finger tip away

How did I get here I wondered

As

I danced on the bridge

How far away the clouds are from me

As the sun shined down on me

I danced around in the green pastures

I looked down and rejoice as I seen the bridge you had

made for me

Sedelia Gardner

Ghetto love

(scene two)

(Prelude)

*Ghetto love just the thought of it soothes my soul as
your scent lingers off in the air and even thou you have
been gone for a while I let your scent wrap my body
and make love to my soul and it feels so good*

*Ghetto love is what I want to share with you because
just the thought of you has me ripened down to the core
and you haven't even touched me yet but everything
inside of me wants you*

*Ghetto love sometimes it can't wait for the bedroom
let me have you right here right now at the door on the
couch on floor or lay me across the table we can stand
up or lay down or bend me over the chair I can't make
it to the bed this act isn't routine it's Ghetto love*

Sedelia Gardner